Walker's American History
series for young people

Who Put the Cannon
in the
Courthouse Square?

Who Put the Cannon in the Courthouse Square?

A Guide to Uncovering the Past

Kay Cooper

Illustrated by Anthony Accardo

Walker and Company
New York

Walker's American History Series for Young People
Frances Nankin, Series Editor

First published in the United States of America in 1984 by the Walker Publishing Company, Inc.

Published simultaneously in Canada by Thomas Allen & Son Canada, Limited, Markham, Ontario

Library of Congress Cataloging in Publication Data

Cooper, Kay.
  Who put the cannon in the courthouse square?

  (Walker's American history series for young people)
  Bibliography: p.
  Includes index.
  Summary: Offers instructions on researching and writing about events in local history. Includes suggestions for projects.
    1. United States—History, Local—Historiography—Juvenile literature. 2. Local history—Juvenile literature. [1. United States—History, Local. 2. Local history] I. Accardo, Anthony, ill. II. Title. III. Series.

E180.C66 1984   973'.072   84-17251

ISBN 0-8027-6547-5
ISBN 0-8027-6561-0 (lib. bdg.)

Book design by Teresa M. Carboni

Printed in the United States of America

10 9 8 7 6 5 4 3

For Wayne, Mary Ellen, and the El Ranchoes
No. 1 and No. 2
(Mary Anne and Kathryn)

cAcknowledgments

The author acknowledges the kind assistance of the following people: Wayne C. Temple, deputy director, Illinois State Archives; Mary Ellen McElligott, editor, *Journal* of the Illinois State Historical Society; Kathryn Ransom, reading coordinator, Springfield Public Schools; Christine Henderson, Library Program Manager One, Illinois State Library; and Alice Lanich, reference librarian, Lincoln Library, all of Springfield, Illinois.

Special thanks also go to Noreen Risko, teacher, Mount Olive High School, Flanders, New Jersey; Frank Puccio, education associate, The New Jersey Historical Society, Newark, New Jersey; David C. DeBoe, director of educational services, The Texas State Historical Association, Austin, Texas; and Tom Belton, executive secretary, Tar Heel Junior Historian Association, Raleigh, North Carolina.

Contents

1

Uncovering the Past in Your Town

IN 1983, THE *Greenville Advocate* published an article titled "Does Anybody Know Where The Cannon Is?" According to the newspaper story, there used to be a big cannon in the courthouse square of Greenville, Illinois. Some sources said it was put there in 1916 by several men who had found it buried three feet under the ground beneath an old chicken house. The men fired the cannon fifteen times to celebrate the re-election of President Woodrow Wilson. Every time the cannon was fired, it made the windows rattle all over town. Later, the cannon was moved into a newspaper office and from there it disappeared.

Since no one in Greenville knew where the cannon was, some people began to think that the big gun had never existed. One such person was a man who had studied Greenville history for many years. When he was contacted to see if he knew anything about the cannon's disappearance, the conversation went something like this:

"So, you're the person who is searching for the cannon. Well, let me tell you that the cannon found in that old chicken house was a toy cannon."

"A toy cannon?"

"Yep! One of those men who found it was James Brown and he'd go all over this county just searching for little things like doorstops and toy cannons."

1

"But I have information that says the cannon was made from a shaft of a water mill, and that it took at least seven men six months to drill a hole in it."

"I don't believe that. My grandmother kept a diary of those days when Wilson was president, and she never mentioned a cannon."

"Really? Well, that is strange. But I can't accept your idea that the cannon was a toy until I have better evidence."

"You want better evidence? I'll give you some. You couldn't get a big cannon into the newspaper office. Only a toy cannon would fit in there."

"How big is a toy cannon?"

"About twelve inches."

"Do you mean that the newspaper office was only a foot long?"

"Oh, no. Ha, ha, ha. It was larger than that. But a big cannon wouldn't fit through the door."

"Well, I've talked to a cannon expert and he claims that the cannon was about four feet long. He says that it was brought to the courthouse square in a car and that it could barely fit inside the backseat. In fact, he's been looking for the Greenville cannon for years."

"Well, he'll never find it! He's searching for something that doesn't exist. That cannon was a toy, I tell you."

Obviously learning the real history of the Greenville cannon will not be an easy task. No one person knows all the facts. No one newspaper article has the complete story. Digging up the real facts will require hard work—work that is almost like police detective work.

For example, when a police detective sets out to solve a crime, he or she starts by looking for clues—facts that point to the criminal. The detective puts all the facts together and tries to solve the crime. If all the facts are there, a complete story is told and the crime is solved. But if facts are missing, the detective cannot put together a complete story. The crime remains unsolved.

Historians—people who study past events and keep a record of all that has happened—also try to piece together a complete story by collecting facts. They are like puzzle solvers putting together an enormous puzzle that is history. They look for all kinds of facts, from those relating to major events to facts about everyday happenings.

Historians are concerned with everyday happenings because they want to know what kind of life-styles people have experienced. What happened to you in school today, for instance, says something about your life. Knowing what your school life is like today helps historians contrast what school life was like for people in the past. In this way historians can see how school life has changed and how it is the same.

Finding out what has happened in the past takes careful and patient detective work. Some of this work is concerned with local history. Local history is the story of what has happened in a particular town or city. It is part of American history. Local history gives fascinating details of important events. It is a history that *you* can help record and preserve.

You can uncover a story about your town by piecing together part of the whole enormous puzzle that is your heritage. What happened to the cannon in the courthouse square of Greenville, Illinois, is part of local history. Maybe your town has a cannon or some other artifact in its courthouse square or park as a reminder of early American life. If you ask a simple question about this artifact, such as "Who put the cannon in the courthouse square?" you will uncover fascinating stories about your town's past.

2

What Is
the Question?

Perhaps you live in a large city such as New York or San Francisco and would like to write about its history. What do you include in a story about your city? The people? Skyscrapers? Art museums? Sports arenas? All are part of your city's history, yet they are too general and too unrelated to make a good story.

Or perhaps you live in a small town and would like to write about its history. What do you include? The people? A church? The town square? Main Street? All make up your town's history, yet these, too, may not fit together to make a good story.

The best way to choose a subject for your story is to select one question you want to ask about your town or city. You might ask, "Why is there a cannon in our courthouse square and who put it there?" Or if you live in San Francisco you might wonder, "How was the Golden Gate Bridge built and who built it?"

By selecting one question, you will have a clear focus for your story. You will be trying to explain one important part of your city or town's local history.

How can you come up with a question? Explore the street on which you live and the area near your school. Walk around for a while and look. What do you see—old buildings, street signs, bridges, a railroad station? What do you know about them? What would you like to know about them? Perhaps your street is called Old Water Pump Street, and there isn't a water pump there. So why is it called Old Water Pump Street? The answer to that question might make a good story.

Or perhaps you've always wondered about an empty canal or a half-buried cemetery. There may be railroad tracks that are no longer used, stone walls in the middle of a woods or an abandoned water tower standing in the countryside. What is the history of this "secret" place? A little detective work might turn up an exciting story.

In fact, every place in your town or city has a history waiting for you to discover. The playground of DuBois School in Springfield, Illinois, for example, was the place where Colonel Ulysses S. Grant and his regiment camped in 1861. Grant later became a general, commanding the Union Army during the Civil War, and served two terms as president of the United States. A story about Grant and his men camping on the school playground would be fascinating, and the topic leads to other questions, such as, "What was it like to be a Civil War soldier?"

Find out if your parents and neighbors lived in your town when they were young. If they did, ask them to tell you about the stores, factories, parks, firehouses and homes they used to visit when they were your age. Are these places still there? If not, what happened to them? Create a question about one of these places, such as, "What was it like to stay overnight in the old hotel?" or "What happened to the bandstand that used to be in the park?"

Another way you might find a good question is by writing down a list of your interests and hobbies. Your list might look something like this:

Interests	Hobbies
horses	piano lessons
	horseback riding lessons
	baseball
	shell collection

Since horses are on the list twice, you might ask a question about the role horses have played in the history of your town or city. Did the early settlers arrive on horseback? Did farmers use horses to work the fields? Is your town or city on an old stagecoach or Pony Express route?

Perhaps you are interested in fire engines. Do you know where the firehouse is? Is there a date on the cornerstone of the building? What citizens first organized the fire company, and how did they raise the money to get the first engine? Where was the first engine bought, how did it operate and what fires did it put out? Working this way, you can think of a lot of questions, and the answers will tell a fascinating story.

What are some other questions you can ask about your town? The list of items that follows will give you some ideas. By reading it, you might think of a question that is just the right one for you to ask.

Ideas for Local History Questions

—Names

How did your town receive its name? Your school? Your street? An old building? Your county? A bridge? A hill? Has the name of your town ever changed? If you live in a subdivision, do all the street names relate to something particular? Names can lead to exciting stories. Marion County, Indiana, for example, was named for Francis Marion, the "Swamp Fox," who was a Revolutionary War hero. Walt Disney thought the story of Francis Marion was so interesting that he made a movie about him titled *The Swamp Fox.*

Does your town or city have a nickname? What does it tell you about its past? Does a certain area in your town or city, such as a hill or a particular neighborhood, have a nickname? What is the history of this place?

—Landmarks

Is there a locomotive in your town? A cannon? A statue? A monument? A bandstand? A canal? A historical marker? A memorial plaque? A fountain in the plaza? A bell in the chapel? A totem pole? One of these places might be the place to begin asking historical questions and to start some interesting detective work.

—Industries

If your town or city is well known for a particular industry, you can investigate the history of that business. Rochester, New York, for example, is known because George Eastman founded Eastman Kodak Company there. Old photographs, newspaper clippings and magazine articles about industries are easy to find in the library. This information will lead you to many historical treasures. A visit to the industry itself will help you complete your story.

—Historical Events

Maybe your town or city is known for an important historical event that happened there. Jarbridge, Nevada, for instance, is known because the last stagecoach robbery in the United States took place near the town on December 5, 1916. (And a stray dog helped lawmen solve the crime!)

—Famous People

Who is the most famous person born or raised in your town or city? An athlete? A politician? A soldier? An artist? Think about writing this person's life story. Ask yourself what this person contributed to American life and how he or she is important to your community.

—Kids One Hundred Years Ago

What sort of life did schoolchildren have in your town a hundred years ago, and how did their life compare with yours? You might want to find out about their school, food, clothes, health and how long the children usually lived. Discover, too, what they did for entertainment.

—Settling In

Why was your town or city settled, and when? Perhaps it started at a crossroad or grew along a river. Who were its first settlers, and why did they come? Why do people come to live there now? What changes have taken place as new people and new industries have arrived?

—Cemeteries

Where is the oldest cemetery in town? Go there and write down in a notebook some of the inscriptions on the tombstones. What do these inscriptions tell you about the people and their lives? What were the causes of death? Are descendants of these people living today? You, as a detective, are going to find the answers to these questions. You might want to record the inscriptions just for infant deaths. Has the number of infant deaths changed over the years? What does this tell you? You may also want to record how many soldiers are buried there, and find out more about one soldier's fight in a battle.

—Wars and Battles

What part did your town or city play in the wars of America? Was a battle fought there? Perhaps people from your town were members of a famous sharpshooter regiment in the Civil War, or maybe someone was a spy. Is there an honor roll monument that lists the names of soldiers who died in battle? Answers to these and other questions will make an exciting story.

—Community Helpers

Who was the first doctor in your community? Where did he or

she live? Who was the first mayor? Milkman? Minister? Blacksmith? Sheriff? What was his or her job like? How long did he or she serve? What were the most interesting parts of the person's job?

—Crime and Punishment

Was there ever a hanging in your town? How have criminals been punished in your town or city since its founding? What was the worst crime in your community's history? The strangest? Where was the first jail? Where is the jail today, and how does it differ from earlier jails?

—Local Lore

Find out if there are any legends, folktales, ballads or songs about the people who live in your community. Lumbermen, cowboys, American Indians, miners and the French of Louisiana are just a few examples of groups who have stories about themselves. An American Indian folktale told in the West, for example, is about an animal that plays ball with its eyes and finally loses them. Such a story could be your history project; and your question could be, "What did this story mean to the Indian tribe that told it?"

—Accidents and Natural Disasters

Has your town or city ever experienced an accident or a natural disaster such as a fire, an explosion, or an earthquake? What persons and businesses were most hurt by the disaster? Did the town and its people change afterward?

—Railroads

Does a railroad pass through or near your community? When was it built? How did your community change when the railroad came? Is there a tunnel through which the train passes? A bridge? What is the history of this structure?

—Automobiles

When and how did the first automobile arrive in your community? Who owned the car? Did the car have a license plate? What did it look like? How did the use of automobiles change your community and the lives of its people?

All these questions and ideas can start you on a fact-finding adventure. When you decide which question or idea interests you the most, go on to Chapter 3.

3

Finding Facts: Strictly Detective Work

Now THAT YOU have your question, how are you going to answer it? What materials do you need? What places should you visit? With whom should you talk? Finding the right source is the whole key to solving the problem. Let's begin with the right materials. Which books, documents and other source materials do you need? And where do you find them?

The best books and documents to use are called original or primary sources. *Original sources* are materials that have been preserved from the period of time you want to study. They include tape-recorded interviews with people who remember historical information and even letters and journals written by people who actually saw historical events. They also include articles from newspapers and other periodicals published at the time. Buildings can be original sources, as well as burial mounds and objects of that time that still exist today.

Three examples of original source materials follow that should give you an idea of how exciting historical sources can be.

This map is from an 1847 journal written by a circuit riding Baptist minister. The journal tells what a circuit rider did each day. A circuit rider was a minister who rode his horse from church to church. The map shows how the countryside north of East Liberty, Ohio, appeared almost 140 years ago. You can see where a schoolhouse was located. The numbers on the right reveal that people measured tracts of land in poles or rods (one rod equals 16½ feet). This map might lead you to ask many questions, such as, What is a sugar camp? Who were the people—the Oarbaughs, the Perkinses, John Smith and William Right—who are mentioned on the map? What happened to them?

The next original source is part of a diary written by Jerry Bryan in a small paper-covered notebook. He carried his notebook from Cordova, Illinois, to the Black Hills of South Dakota and back again in 1897. His writings reveal many facts about western mining communities. For example, there seems to have been an Indian raid near Crook City around August 1. Why would there have been an Indian raid? Was the land Indian country? If so, why were white people there? Answers to these questions can be found by reading Bryan's diary.

The diary also states that "Wild Bill" was shot. Research in a library will reveal that "Wild Bill" was James Butler Hickok, a famous United States marshal. Why was he there? If you do more research, you'll find that Hickok apparently was financing gold prospectors, hoping that one of them would "strike it rich." These men in Deadwood were tough, while Bryan was scared to death. Do you think Deadwood had a law office, sheriff or court? You, as a detective, can find out.

On August 2, 1897, Bryan wrote in his diary:

An exciting day in Dead Wood. The fun commenced early this morning by a crowd of twenty armed men escorting a murderer through town. This fellow had killed his man in Gay Ville two miles above this. Some three or four weeks ago he was caught at Fort Laramie, brought back and tried yesterday in Gay Ville and turned loose and was guarded through town this morning. About noon a man was found just across the creek dead—cause of death: poor whiskey. Just after dinner Wild Bill was shot through the head and killed instantly. While the crowd was debating whether to hang the assassin or not, reports came from Crook City that the Indians have surrounded the town and that help was wanted. All those that could get horses went down to render assistance.

It is getting too dangerous here to be healthy. A man is liable to be shot here any time by some drunken desperado. And it is not safe to go out, but we have decided to go tomorrow. Anything is better than staying here. We have secured passage to Fort Pierre. All we have to do is to start, and fight our way through if necessary. We have good guns—none better—plenty of munitions of war. No very good feeling for Mr. Lo, anyhow, so here goes.*

*Excerpt from "Trip To And From The Hills," by Jerry Bryan, in *An Illinois Gold Hunter in the Black Hills*, the Illinois State Historical Society, 1960.

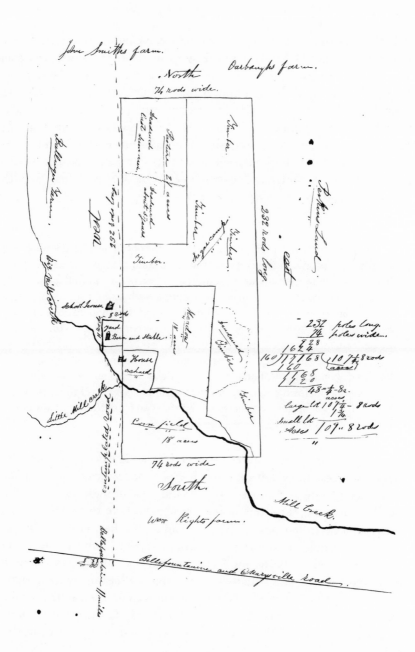

From the Journal of Elder William Fuson, a circuit riding Baptist minister, Courtesy of the Ohio Historical Society, Inc.

J. H. Buckingham, a reporter for the *Boston Courier* in Massachusetts, recorded his trip to Chicago and the West in 1847. He traveled by stage and steamer, describing the towns he saw, the inns in which he slept and the people he met. His description of a circus performing in Keokuk, Iowa, helps you to understand what people were like in the past and what they did for entertainment. As a detective, you might try to find out if in 1847, fifty cents was an inexpensive or an expensive admission fee for a circus. You also might ask yourself how today's circus performances compare with Mr. Buckingham's experience at the circus. What does the answer tell you about how people change?

Buckingham wrote:

> A circus company was performing here this afternoon; and for the purpose of seeing the people of the country, I went to their tent, at the expense of fifty cents. There were about six hundred people present, of all ages, sizes and descriptions, mostly women and children, with a slight sprinkling of a country dandy or so, and it was amusing to witness their expressions of feeling at the performances. So far as the circus company was concerned, the performances were the poorest I ever saw, and the horses and the band appeared to be about equally stupid; but the audience was not only a delighted, but a delightful one — everybody was happy, and everybody was astonished; the clown could not make too stupid a joke, and the man who turned three somersaults was pronounced the wonder of the age. How easy and how cheap it is to make people happy!*

Secondary sources are materials written by people who have studied the original sources. Encyclopedias and books about your county and state are secondary sources. You may want to use some of these sources in your research, and Chapter 4 tells you more about where to look for them.

As you know from reading about the cannon in the courthouse square, records and people often disagree on what happened, why and to whom. Whenever you find conflicting facts, you must act as the judge and jury do in court and decide which person or record has an opinion that is closest to the truth. The best way to decide is to go back to the original source and try to understand it. The closer you get to the original source, the more likely you are to uncover the facts that bring you nearer the truth.

*Excerpt from "Illinois As Lincoln Knew It: A Boston Reporter's Record of a Trip in 1847," Harry E. Pratt, editor, *Papers in Illinois History and Transactions of the Illinois State Historical Society*, 1937. Courtesy of the Illinois State Historical Society.

How to Find Facts

There are six basic steps involved in locating your original and secondary source materials. Follow these steps and you will be on your way to becoming an excellent detective.

1. Tell everyone you know what you are working on. You'll be amazed at how many people will be willing to help you, and surprised by what and whom they know.
2. Ask questions. If the first person doesn't know the answer, then ask someone else. If you think someone might have the information you need, write or call that person and explain your needs clearly and simply.
3. Be polite, but don't take no for an answer. It's your duty to get the facts!
4. Let your question guide your research. Read every scrap of material you can find that deals with your question.
5. Keep alert. It may be a small detail that leads you to the best parts of your story.
6. Reason from what you have found. If you think something is not quite right, check your facts. If you find conflicting facts, try to discover from which sources the facts came.

Sometimes when there are conflicting facts, it turns out that all the facts are true. The nickname given to a town, for example, could have come from many sources. These sources may tell different stories about the nickname and, in fact, all may be equally true. Thus, you can write about all the various nickname stories.

In the process of searching for facts, look out for prejudices. For example, if you are trying to find out who lived in your neighborhood at a particular time, you might look at the United States Census Manuscripts for that specific year. In certain parts of the country, Native Americans were discriminated against. American Indian women married to white men were listed in the census as housekeepers instead of wives. (For more about U.S. Census Manuscripts, see chart in Chapter 4. Look under heading Community Helpers.)

Wherever you look for facts, do take notes. Use either 3×5 cards or a steno notebook. Write a few words at the top of the card or page stating the subject of your notes. For instance, if you want to find out about a famous person in your community, your card or page might be headed "Birthplace." Or if you are uncovering facts about a local landmark, your note or page might be headed "People Involved with the Project." These key words will help you organize your facts as you uncover them. Use one note card or notebook page for each important fact.

Under your key words, write down where you found the source, in what library and in what file. This information will help you find the source again, in case you want to check a fact.

Next, write down the title of the source, the author's last name and the page numbers you used. This information will help you prepare your footnotes, in case you want to use them.

Under this, write down whatever the author says that helps to answer your question. Stick with the subject listed at the top of your card or page, and either quote the author directly or use your own words to tell as accurately as possible what the author has said.

As you take notes, list every source you use on a separate sheet of paper or in another notebook. This list is your working bibliography and should contain the following information:

For a Book

1. Author's name, last name first. Record the editor's name in the same way if there is an editor instead of an author.
2. Title of book. Include volume number, if needed.
3. Publication facts. Include the place where the book was published, the publisher's name, the date the book was published.

Examples

Loeb, Robert H., Jr. *Meet the Real Pilgrims.* New York: Doubleday & Company, Inc., 1979.

Siegel, Beatrice. *Fur Trappers and Traders: The Indians, the Pilgrims, and the Beaver.* New York: Walker and Company, 1981.

For a Magazine or Journal Article

1. Author's name, last name first.
2. Title of article.

3. Title of magazine or journal, volume number, date of issue, page references.

Examples

Snow, Richard F. "The Battlefield at Gettysburg." American Heritage Society's *Americana*. Vol. 1, (July 1973), pp. 2–7. (Notice that the abbreviation used for more than one page is "pp." The abbreviation used for a single page is "p.")

West, Elizabeth. "Fifty Years At Lime Rock." *Cobblestone*. Vol. 2, (June 1981), pp. 10–15.

Let's Talk to a Historian

A resource you're going to find helpful as you look for answers to your question is a local historian. Your teacher or a librarian may know a historian in a nearby college who will talk to your class. Or you can look in the White Pages of the telephone book under the heading "Historical Society." A historical society has historical information, and a historian there may be able to help you.

When you talk to the historian, you might say something like this:

"Hello. My name is Jeff Johnston and I'm working on a local history project. I wonder if you could help me with a couple of questions. I want to know who put the cannon in the courthouse square. Can you suggest any places where I might find the answer to that question?"

If the historian suggests places to search for the answer, make sure you write them down.

Don't be upset, however, if the historian tells you that your question can't be answered. Some records have been destroyed in fires or simply lost. For example, the original architectural drawing of your town's first jail might be missing. So if your question is "What did my town's first jail look like?", you'll have problems coming up with a complete answer. If you reword your question and ask, "What has my town's jail looked like in the past?", you may have better luck.

Now that you have an idea about the kinds of books, documents and other source materials you are going to need, you are ready to go on to the following chapters.

4

Looking It Up in the Library

TELLING SOMEONE HOW to use the library is almost like telling Marco Polo how to explore China or where to find gold. You use two rules:

1. Go there.
2. Explore.

Types of Libraries

Libraries are some of the best places to search for local history information. Your own school library may have books about your topic as well as about the history of your town and state, and your local public library has books and materials that should be useful to you. If the materials you think you need are not part of the public library's collection, the librarian can borrow them for you from libraries throughout the United States. Every state also has a state library, located in the capital city, which has books about your state's history and culture, including books and documents about your particular town or city.

In addition, every state has a state historical library, located either in the state capital or in the city where the leading college or university is. This library collects manuscripts, books, maps and pictures about the state. It may also have the state's old newspapers on microfilm (a strip of film on which the pages of the paper are photographed in miniature). Newspapers are original source materials.

Libraries are also found in museums, universities, banks, historical societies, law offices, business offices for industries and medical societies. Some of these are special libraries because their materials cover only a particular type of information, but many have materials on local history. The library in your state or town historical society, for example, may have letters, diaries and other documents that have to do with your community's history.

Asking the Librarian for Help

Keep in mind that one of your best resources for information is the librarian. He or she can help you find the materials you need. Tell the librarian what you are working on, and make it plain what you want to know. Ask specific questions, such as, "Where can I find . . . ?" The librarian will be willing to help you.

How to Use the Library

You've probably noticed that library books are marked with numbers and letters, usually on the book's spine. What does this mean?

Every library has a classification system, a way of keeping its books in a specific place and in precise order. The numbers and letters on the book's spine are the "call numbers" of the system. By using call numbers, any book in the library can be found.

Libraries use two main classification systems. One is the Dewey Decimal Classification System; the other is the Library of Congress Classification System (LC).

In the Dewey Decimal System, any call number in the 900s is in the category of history. In the LC System, any book with a call number beginning with E or F is in the class of American history.

So how do you find the books you need to answer your question? All the library's books are listed in a catalog kept in the library. The catalog usually consists of small, separate cards kept in a cabinet of drawers. Thus it is called the *card catalog*. The card catalog has been organized according to the library's classification system, and the call numbers appear above each book listed, typed in one of the upper corners of the cards.

It's your job to search through the catalog to find the books you need. Then copy the call numbers of the books accurately on the call slips furnished by the library. In some libraries you will have to turn these slips in to the library desk, and the librarian will use the numbers to get the books you want. In other libraries, however, you must get the books yourself. If it is a very big library, the call numbers of the system and the location of the shelves are posted on a map that should be near the card catalog. Locate your call number on the map and go to that section of the library. The shelves will be marked with guide labels.

Reference Books

Many of the books you will need to answer your question are reference books. Reference books cannot be checked out. You must go to the library and use them there. Reference books are kept in a special place in the library—a reference section or reference room.

The list of reference books that follows includes only a few of the thousands of books that are available. Read through the list to see how many different kinds of reference books there are. Most are secondary sources. One may help you with your question.

Finding the Right Reference Book and Record

If Your Question Is About:	Find This Book or Document:	It Will Give You:
Community helpers	City or telephone directories from the time period you are working with.	A list of all the town's adult residents, their addresses and jobs. They often contain advertisements that reveal much about the business, economy and social life of past years.
	U.S. Census Manuscripts. *Note:* A census is taken every ten years, so don't try to find information about your town's people in 1845, for example, by looking for these records.	The names of people, their addresses, occupations and information about their families. Your public library can rent microfilm copies of the 1790–1910 census records for $2.25 per roll. (The 1890 census was destroyed by fire.)
Famous people	*Biography and Genealogy Master Index*, Dennis La Beau and Gary C. Tarbert, editors. 8 volumes. Detroit, Michigan: Gale Research Co., 1975.	"Who's Who" directories. This is an index. It directs you to the biography that will tell you about the life of the person you are seeking.
	Your state bluebook (a set of volumes called bluebooks because the books were bound in blue covers when first published. Later editions come in any color.)	Biographical sketches of important people in your state government. Contains an article about your state library's collection. Read this article to discover if the library has any materials

you need. The address of the library is at the end of the article. There is a section in this book that tells you how to write to the library.

Kids 100 years ago	*Historic Dress in America, 1607–1800*, by Elisabeth McClellan. Philadelphia: George W. Jacobs & Co., 1904.	Examples of dress in the Spanish and French settlements of Florida and Louisiana, and dress in the English colonies during this period.
	Here Was the Revolution, Historic Sites of the War for American Independence, by Harlan D. Unrau. Washington, D.C.: National Park Service, 1976.	A description of historic sites and buildings associated with the war.
Landmarks	*The National Register of Historic Places*, Ronald M. Greenberg, editor. Washington, D.C.: U.S. National Park Service, 1976.	Short sketches of historical buildings.
	Encyclopedia of Black America, W. Augustus Low, editor. New York: McGraw-Hill, 1981.	Black folklore and the history of black newspapers. Contains a bibliography.
Local lore	*The Rainbow Book of American Folk Tales and Legends*, by Maria Leach. New York: The World Publishing Company, 1958.	Collections of tales and legends, with many illustrations.

(continued on next page)

	Stories and ballads connected with the Mississippi River. The book contains an index of authors, titles and first lines of songs, and of subjects, names and places.
A Treasury of Mississippi River Folklore, by Benjamin A. Botkin. New York: Crown Publishers, Inc., 1955.	
Names	
The American Counties, by Joseph N. Kane. Metuchen, N.J.: The Scarecrow Press, 1983	The origin of county names. The introduction is fascinating because it answers such questions as "For whom has the greatest number of counties been named?"
American Place-Names, by George Stewart. New York: Oxford, 1970.	The meaning and origin of many American names. For example, it tells you that the first Springfield was in Massachusetts and named after a village in England.
Illustrated Dictionary of Place Names, by Kelsie B. Harder. New York: Van Nostrand Reinhold Co., 1976.	The origin, meaning and historic importance of names. For example, the name Detroit (Michigan) is the French word for *strait*. The early settlement was named Detroit because it was located on a strait that lies between Lake Erie and St. Clair Lake.
County histories (one or more volumes).	Information about the founders of each town in your county and about each
Settling in	

Historical atlases (bound collections of maps, charts and tables). — town's early history. They also may give you a history of the cannon in the courthouse square and tell you why a monument is important to a town's history.

The Reader's Encyclopedia of the American West, Howard R. Lamar, editor. New York: Thomas Y. Crowell, 1977. — Old plans of cities, locations of American Indian tribes at specific times in history, maps showing the battles and headquarters of forces in America's wars and the movement of people across the United States.

Historic sites, language, the arts, trade, discovery, exploration, people and places of the Old West.

Wars and Battles

The American Heritage Picture History of the Civil War, Richard Ketchum, editor. New York: American Heritage Publishing Company, 1960. — Information about America from 1860 to 1865. Two volumes plus a chronology pamphlet that lists battles and gives short biographical sketches of important people in the war.

Encyclopedia of the American Revolution, by Mark Mayo Boatner III. New York: David McKay Company, Inc., 1974. — Information about America from 1763 to 1783. Includes cross-references, maps, biographical sketches and a bibliography.

Vertical Files

Do not forget to search for your subject in the vertical file, which is found in most libraries and is usually a file cabinet with several drawers. The outsides of the drawers are labeled with alphabetical guide letters. In the drawers are folders packed with pictures, newspaper clippings, pamphlets and brochures filed under different subjects. These folders are kept in an upright position; thus the file is called *vertical*. Near the file is an index to the material, which lists the subjects or topics to be found there.

Vertical files are always full of surprises. The file in the Illinois State Historical Library was where the Greenville cannon story was first found. It was in a folder marked "Cannons." A reference to the cannon was also found in a folder labeled "Courthouse."

Newspapers and Photographs

One of the best local history sources to be found in your public library is your local newspaper. It is the diary of your town, telling day by day what has happened.

Some libraries have newspapers going back more than one hundred years. When you look through old newspapers, search for articles written by local historians and for special issues that were published to celebrate anniversaries of your town's or city's beginning. Glance through advertisements to see what people wore and what they could buy in stores or from mills and workshops.

Study old photographs and discover how much your town has changed. "Read" the photograph as you would a book, from left to right, then downward. Study the photograph several times, and each time try to find something you've missed.

You may want to keep a record of each photograph. You can do this in a notebook. At the top of the page, write down the place and date of the photo. Under this, write down where you found it. Next list all the facts about the photo that you can see, including people, animals, plants and objects. Describe the mood of the photograph. Do the people look happy, sad, bored, formal? Can you find out why? Attach a copy of the photo to your record. You can make a copy of the photo in the library.

Deadwood, Dakota Territory, 1876.
Photo courtesy of the Nebraska State Historical Society, Lincoln, Nebraska.

Write down all the facts about the photo that you can see, such as those listed below.

Four stores shown:

1. C.H. Sheldon. Sign outside store says Gold Dust Bought. Bulletin board with items posted. Some sort of large table outside. Wooden step up to store. Glass in windows and door. Two-story structure. Upper part may be storage area. Boards on stores travel vertically. Why?
2. J.W. Watkin & Co. Similar in structure to Sheldon store.
3. Kurtz ? & Co. Similar in structure to Sheldon store.
4. ? no name appears in photo. One-story structure, made of wood.

Other objects and observations:

> Pine trees on hill. Is town built in a valley?
> Boards on right of photo.
> Outdoor sign on left?
> Dirt street.

People: Men dressed in high boots, hats, overcoats (so it's probably cold). Many men have beards. One may be smoking a corncob pipe. Looks as if there's a woman behind the man in the white shirt. Man at far left may be Mexican. All men appear to be about the same age. All are dressed in casual working clothes.

Mood of photo: People look bored and tired. Standing around as if had nothing better to do. Why? Do they want to go home, or are they tired of standing still for the photographer?

Writing to the State Historical Library or Special Libraries

If a library has materials you need, you can write to the library and ask for them. The library will make copies of the materials and send them to you.

If you write to your state historical library, ask questions that begin with *who, what, when, where, how* or *why*. You might write, "I am trying to find the answers to these questions: Why did people settle in my town? Who were they? How did they earn a living?"

It's a good idea to let the librarian know what you already have discovered about your subject. You might write, "I know how William Penn founded my city—Philadelphia—but I need information about his childhood. Would you send me some information about Penn's early life?"

Do not ask the librarian to send you everything the library has on your subject. The library probably would have to hire a truck to haul all the information to you.

In the back of this book is a directory that will help you find the addresses and phone numbers of libraries that may be helpful to you. Also, for information about your state historical library, check your state bluebook. (For more about bluebooks, see Famous People in the chart about reference books.)

5

Places to Visit

WHERE ELSE CAN you go to get the answer to your question? There may be places you can visit that will have original source materials related to your subject. Some of the following places might be helpful.

Museums

Perhaps you've found an arrowhead in your backyard and would like to know how it got there. You're thinking that maybe Indians once camped on your land and that some might be buried there. How do you find out?

One way is to visit a museum in or near your town or city. A list of museums is in the Yellow Pages of your telephone book under the heading "Museums." It is a good idea to call the museum before you visit it and ask if it has information dealing with your question.

Museums exhibit every "old thing" imaginable, from Indian relics to Civil War weapons. Arrowheads similar to yours may be in an exhibit. A history of the Indians who made them may be printed in a pamphlet or booklet. And a map of Indian camps in your area may even be posted on the wall!

Talk to the curator of the museum or to one of the guides. He or she may know a lot about Indians, or know someone who does.

Or perhaps you are interested in finding out how some famous person lived in your neighborhood during a specific time in history. Visiting an old house that has been turned into a museum is one way to see how that person lived. For example, you can visit the home of Louisa May Alcott in Concord, Massachusetts, and see where *Little Women* was written. The house and its contents allow you to see how the writer and her family lived in that neighborhood during the 1860s.

Historical Societies

The shelves of state and local historical societies are usually packed with letters, scrapbooks, old books, pictures and maps of your city or town. Some historical societies have exhibits where, for example, your community's first fire engine and first newspaper might be displayed. In addition to finding answers to your question, you are sure to find treasures in the historical society you might otherwise overlook.

You may even discover that the society has developed or is in the process of developing local history projects. The Colorado State Historical Society in Denver, for instance, has put together several "Grandmother Trunks." Each is a real trunk, made sometime around 1900. Each has been lined with paper that was made in the 1900s and filled with items that a real grandmother might have saved at that time. For variety, each trunk represents a grandmother of a particular ethnic group, including blacks, Cheyennes, Italians, and Mexican-Americans.

Patriotic Organizations

Was your community at any time the scene of a battle? Keep in mind that several wars have been fought in the United States: the American Revolution, the French and Indian Wars, the Civil War, the War of 1812 and the Mexican War or Texas Revolution, to name a few.

If you are searching for information about a battle, find out if there are any local patriotic organizations in your town by asking at your historical society for the names of these organizations. Then look up the name in the White Pages of the telephone book under the organization's name, such as Daughters of the American Revolution, Daughters of the Republic of Texas and the American Legion.

Call the organization and ask the person answering the phone if the organization has any information on a specific battle or war. The group might have a small museum exhibiting weapons, uniforms and sketches of the battle. Brochures about a battle or war might be there, too. In addition, the organization may have representatives who will come to your school and tell about your town's part in our country's military history.

Churches and Synagogues

Is your church or synagogue one of the oldest in the county? If it is, you may want to find out about its history. If it is not, you may want to record its history before many of the facts about it are lost.

The information you will need is in the minutes kept by the trustees or in the earliest congregational records. Ask your clergyman or clergywoman if you can read the oldest records. If this work is complete, you should discover when the building was constructed, what it cost, who paid for it and who donated materials for the construction.

As you research for facts, you may discover that someone has already written a history of the building. Such a discovery will help you. Read through it, but take notes from the actual records. You might discover something that the other writer overlooked and uncover new information.

You never know what your search will reveal. One researcher found that his congregation used to hold trials. During the 1700s on Nantucket Island, Massachusetts, trials were held by Quakers for members who disobeyed the Quaker moral code and discipline. Members were brought to trial for attending dances, going to oyster parties and walking along the wharf.

Schools

What were the schools and teachers like in your town a hundred years ago?

In 1877, one school superintendent visited schools in Scott County, Illinois, and kept a record of his visits. "Too much tobacco chewing and spitting on the floor," he wrote about one teacher. "Methods of teacher good, except she talks too much and is too cross," was another comment.

Where can you find information like this? You can find it by searching in old school records, which might be filed away in a historical society, university archive or county courthouse. People working in your local school district office might be able to tell you where the records are most likely to be found. The records may be in the school office.

Facts from school records will reveal the names of the children who went to the school and will give each pupil's birth date, race, religion, names of family members, occupations of parents and address. From this information, you will have gathered enough clues to lead you to many other sources as your story unfolds.

State Archives

Do you live on a street named for a Civil War general? Do you want to find out more about one soldier's fight in a battle? Was the most famous person born or raised in your town a soldier? If so, you might want to get a copy of this person's military service record. To do this, write a letter to your State Archives and request the record. The archives, located in your capital city, houses all government-related documents. When you request the record, you may receive a form to fill out. Complete the form, return it and a copy of the record will be sent to you.

Military service records reveal interesting facts. A Civil War record, for instance, will give a soldier's height, complexion, color of hair, color of eyes, race and age, and will tell if he was wounded, killed or captured. The soldier's residence at the time of his enlistment is given, too.

Cemeteries

Another place to visit is an old cemetery, because history is recorded on gravestones.

Symbols or designs and pictures carved into stones usually tell about the religion and religious beliefs of the people buried there. For example, skeleton heads called death's-heads were carved on gravestones when the

The records of the Adjutant General's Office, now in the State
Archives, show the following Civil War service record on:

Name: *Duncan J. Hall*　　　Rank: *Captain*

Unit: *Co. A, 89th Inf. Regt., Ill. Vols.*

Age: *24*　　　Height: *5'6"*　　　Hair: *Brown*

Eyes: *Hazel*　　Complexion: *Light*

Marital Status: *Single*　　Occupation: *Lawyer*

Nativity:
Town: *Detroit*　　County:　　State: *Michigan*

Joined for Service and Enrolled
When: *July 23, 1862*　　　Where: *Chicago, Ill.*

By whom: *himself*　　　Term: *3 years*

Mustered into Service
When: *Aug. 25, 1862*　　　Where: *Chicago, Ill.*

By whom: *Capt. Christopher*

Residence
Town: *Chicago*　　County: *Cook*　　State: *Ill.*

Mustered Out
When:　　　　Where:

By whom:

REMARKS: *(n.do Promoted Lt. Col.) Promoted Major, Feb. 2½, 1863, Murfreesboro, Tenn. Killed in battle of Chickamauga, Ga., Sept. 20, 1863.*

AR D-48.2

Puritan religion was common in New England during the sixteenth and seventeenth centuries. Puritans saw death as a time when people were seriously judged by an angry God. By the early eighteenth century, New Englanders viewed death as a time when people were judged by a loving and forgiving God. Thus, angel heads were carved on tombstones.

The writing or inscription on a grave usually gives the name and birth and death dates of the person buried there. Some old inscriptions also give the names of the dead person's parents or children, the dead person's place of birth and marriage date.

If you find many stones with the same death date on them, check a local newspaper for that day to see what happened. There may have been an epidemic such as an outbreak of cholera, a natural disaster such as a tornado or an accident such as a fire, which took several lives.

Don't be surprised if you cannot find the graves of early pioneers. These people may have died before stonecutters came to your community, so no stone ever marked their graves. Wooden markers may have been used and were never replaced when they rotted away.

For your records, you can make rubbings of gravestones. All you need is an ordinary wax crayon, a roll of masking tape and a sheet of thick paper. Shelf paper works well. Stretch the paper over the surface of the stone and hold it securely in place with tape. (If the paper shifts, the image will be blurred.) Gently rub the paper with the crayon until an image appears. You can rub harder to make the details darker.

In some cemeteries, however, rubbings are not permitted because constant rubbing wears down the stone or brass. So it's a good idea to get permission from the cemetery office before you do rubbings. Sometimes a fee is charged.

Other Places

Battlefields, forts, lighthouses and restoration villages are some of the other places you can visit. If your question leads you to one of these sites, go there and learn about it.

During your visit, look for small museums, plaques, maps on the walls of visitor centers and brochures. Guides are often there to help you, so ask them questions. Carry a notebook in which you have written questions you think you might want to ask. You also might want to carry a camera and record in the notebook information about each photograph you take. If you do plan to take pictures, practice using your camera before your trip.

Places to Go to Find the Right Record

If Your Question Is About:	And You Need to Find:	Go to:	Clues and Warnings!
Community helpers	A will	The County Circuit Clerk's office in the county building or courthouse. To find the county building, look up the name of your county in the White Pages of the phone book. Directly under the name is the address of the county building.	
Famous people	A death or birth certificate	The County Clerk's office, located in the county building.	Call the office first and tell the person that you are a student working on a local history project. Explain that you need a death or birth certificate. The person in the office will tell you if he or she can search for the record and make a copy of it. The person might ask you to come to the office and fill out an

(continued on next page)

39

application for the record and pay a research fee of about $3. If you can't get to the office, ask the person to mail the application to you. *Warning!* Some county clerks do not have indexes for records and may not want to search for the certificate. In this case, you might want to ask your parents or teacher to help you. Don't give up until you have a copy of it!

| Landmarks | Which buildings in your town are important to its past | For information, write to your State Department of Conservation (located in your state capital) and the National Register, National Park Service, Washington, D.C. 20240. |
| Settling in | Old maps of your town | The public library, state historical library, state library. It may be possible to get a photocopy of those sections of large maps that include your town. You also can write |

Wars and Battles		
An American Revolutionary War record	Your state historical library.	Look for the D.A.R. (Daughters of the American Revolution) *Lineage Books.* First check the indexes to the volumes for the soldier's name. The indexes will direct you to the precise book in which the soldier's life story appears. Also see the section about writing to your state historical library in Chapter 4.
		to the U.S. Geological Survey, NCIC, 507 National Center, Reston, Virginia 22092, for an aerial photograph showing your town and the area around it. The price for a black-and-white photo is about $9.
Civil War record	Your state or the national archives.	Read the section on the State Archives in Chapter 4. Also see the Directory in the back of this book for the address of the National Archives.

6

People
to Interview

$\mathcal{A}$NOTHER WAY YOU can get some answers to your question is by talking to people — your parents, grandparents and other older people in your community — who actually were involved in some way with your topic.

Your family, the alumni of your school and the people of your community have probably taken part in some of your town's local history and perhaps even in the country's most important events, such as a war.

Don't be afraid to interview a great-uncle whom you hardly know or someone you don't know at all. Most people will be pleased by your interest in them and probably will give you good information. Some may know local folklore — tales of ghosts, witches, old sayings, ballads and old beliefs. Others may have old letters and diaries that contain historical information. If the person has any old letters or diaries, ask him or her to let you read them. Explain that you are trying to discover a more truthful picture of the past and that these original source materials will help you, just as the interview will.

Before the interview, think about what questions you want to ask and make a list of these in a notebook. You can either call the person on the phone to conduct the interview or arrange to meet the person at a place approved by your parents or teacher. If you don't know the person you want to interview, you might begin your conversation by saying something like this:

"Hello. Are you Mrs. Smith? Yes? Well, I'm Sarah Brown. You may have heard of my family. My dad owns the furniture store at Twelfth and Elm. I'm John Brown's granddaughter. Well, I'm working on a story about our town's first streetcar, and everywhere I've gone people ask me if I've talked to you. I understand you rode in a trailer that was a streetcar and that it was pulled by mules. If you have some time, I'd like to talk to you about your ride."

Beginning like this, you probably will have your interview. If not, you can say something like, "But I'm really interested in finding out about the streetcar, and you know so much about it."

If the person you want to interview refuses to talk to you, you must politely thank him or her and then try to get the information from someone else. If the person does want to talk to you, however, listen carefully to what the person says and take notes. Have several pencils with you (in case one breaks) and your notebook.

During the conversation, you may find that the person you are interviewing talks about things that have nothing to do with your subject. It's your job to get that person back on the topic by saying, "You know, I really was interested in what you said a few moments ago. Could you tell me more about that?"

Some tips to help you conduct your interview:

1. Don't ask questions that can be answered with yes or no. Start with words such as *why, when, what kind of, how much was,* and *where did that happen*.
2. Ask one question at a time. Make your questions brief and simple.
3. Don't let periods of silence bother you. Give the person plenty of time to think about his or her answers.
4. Don't rush from question to question.
5. Don't interrupt a good story because you've suddenly thought of

a question. Jot down your question in your notebook and ask it later.

6. Don't be afraid to ask for more information to help you clearly understand what the person means. Try to find out the dates, locations and names of the people involved in a story.
7. Don't let the interview go on for more than an hour and a half. If you need more time, a return visit or telephone conversation can be arranged.

After the interview, immediately go over your notes and write down what the person said in as much detail as possible. Then check again any facts that you are uncertain about by calling the person you interviewed on the phone or by doing more research.

History on Tape

If you have a tape recorder, you can collect information on tape. Before you do the interview, practice using the tape recorder with your friends and family members. Choose any subject of mutual interest and develop a series of questions about it. Then interview the friend or family member. After the interview, listen to the tape and pick out sections that are good and bad. Do another interview and try to improve it.

Some tips to help you in a tape-recorded interview:

1. Use the best quality tapes you can afford and an external rather than a built-in microphone (if you have one).
2. Interview the person in a quiet place.
3. Don't switch the recorder off and on.
4. Sometimes people become bashful and won't talk when the tape recorder is switched on. To help them relax, ask them to get something they had as a child and talk about it. Perhaps they have an old school dress, a sampler made by a relative or a portrait. Ask them how long they've had the object and why

they have kept it. Once the person is talking, you can go on with your interview.

5. Use the tips for interviewing mentioned earlier in this chapter.

After the interview, have the person sign a form that gives you permission to use the tape for your subject. The form should look something like this:

Decatur High School: Local History

I hereby give my permission to the history class of Decatur High School to use this interview for educational purposes as the class shall determine. The tape recordings and their contents are listed below:

_____

Name of Person Being Interviewed

_____

Address

_____

Name of Interviewer

_____

Date of Agreement

_____

Subject(s) of Tape(s)

If you make your interview available to other historical researchers, your interview then becomes *oral history*. You can do this by donating the tapes to a library or by writing out the interview and publishing it.

7

Writing
Your Story

Now that you have your question, have found your sources and have gathered all the information you can find in answer to your question, how are you going to write your story?

First ask yourself, "Did I really answer my question? Are there still things unexplained?" If there are, you may need to do more research.

Before you begin writing, organize your notes by subject, or perhaps chronologically. Then do an outline. Outlines force you to organize your thoughts so your ideas follow in order. And they let you see how your story will start, what will be in the middle and how it will end.

How do you begin an outline? Ask yourself these questions: "What part of my story do I like best? What interests me most about it?" This interesting part can be the beginning of your outline.

A junior high school pupil whose question was "What was Crow's Mill School like when it was a rural schoolhouse?" began her outline by describing the feeling she had when she rode her bicycle past the school. An outline for her story (which appears at the end of this chapter), follows.

Crow's Mill School

1. Observing the school
   a) How I feel when I pass the school
   b) What I hear coming from the school
2. Location of the school
   a) In my neighborhood
   b) Today's exact location
   c) Past location
3. History of the school
   a) When and where first built
   b) Why named Crow's Mill
   c) School moved in 1933
      1. New location
      2. New name
      3. Who went there
      4. Names of teachers who taught there
   d) Closing of the school
      1. Why it closed
      2. Where pupils went to school
4. School becomes Navy Club
5. School is restored

With an outline as the basis for your story, you can begin writing. As you write, don't worry about the spelling, punctuation and grammar. You can correct those later. Just get the words down on paper!

Don't be afraid to change your outline as you write. You may find that a few numbers need to be switched so that your story is better organized.

The hardest part of writing is those first few words. Read the opening sentences of stories and articles to get yourself going. Here are a few examples of opening paragraphs written by junior and senior high school pupils.

In 1971, my family moved to a small farm at the head of a valley in western North Carolina. I was four years old. This farm had long been called Dock

Fox place, and I understand that the first people settled this land in the 1820s and 1830s.

As my brother and I played on our land, we found chips of flint and pottery shards in certain areas. An idea formed and grew into curiosity about other people who may have lived here. We found large pieces of pottery in a nearby swamp. One particular piece showed the finger imprints of the person who made it. As my fingers ran where hers had, I wondered about who had lived on this land before the white settlers. . . .

(From "A Pisgah Woman: What She Represents on Our Farm," by Ingrid Brunk, Barnardsville School, Barnardsville, North Carolina, in *Tar Heel Junior Historian,* Fall 1980.)

The days of the blue-uniformed lighthouse keeper, who checked his whale oil supply and slowly climbed the tower to clean his lenses, have passed forever. Yet the lighthouse he so faithfully attended remains on duty. Two hundred and eight feet tall and dressed in a distinctive pattern of spiraling black-and-white stripes, the Cape Hatteras Lighthouse stands near a spot still dreaded by mariners. Its needle of light still guides them as it has for a hundred years. . . .

(From "Cape Hatteras Lighthouse," by Lori Pait, Hamlet Junior High School, Hamlet, North Carolina, in *Tar Heel Junior Historian,* Spring 1983.)

The small stone house located on Flanders-Drakestown Road in Flanders, New Jersey, was thought to be a pump house. There is a small stone bearing the inscription "LPC 1855." The initials were first thought to stand for Lakeland Pump Company and the date was thought to be the founding date. . . .

(From "We Thought It Was a Pump House, But Evidence Points Otherwise," by Jessica Shotwell, Mount Olive High School, Flanders, New Jersey, 1983 unpublished.)

On November 6, 1981, I interviewed Mr. King Williams. Mr. Williams, an educator, was born in Blount's Creek, North Carolina. He is eighty-three years old, and he has a very vivid memory. He was wearing his bathrobe while sitting in a large, comfortable chair. His wife was sitting opposite him in a recliner. I could see around the room the various trophies Mr. Williams had been awarded. As I turned on my tape recorder, I felt that I was about to have an experience that would be fun. . . .

(From "Mr. King Williams, An Educator," by Scott Perry, Perquimans County Union School, Winfall, North Carolina, in *Tar Heel Junior Historian,* Fall 1982.)

Once your opening sentences are written, read the words over carefully. Did you write exactly what you wanted to say? Have you introduced your subject? Will your reader understand what you meant?

Ask a few friends to read your opening sentences and to tell you in their own words what they have read. If they are not sure about what you meant to say, then you should rewrite the beginning of your story.

Writers, even famous ones, rewrite. Sometimes they rewrite one paragraph twenty or more times. Rewriting is the whole key to writing. It is the only way you can make clear what you really want to say. So don't hesitate to cross out words and sentences as you work to improve your writing.

When your opening sentences say exactly what you meant them to say and in such a way that your reader clearly understands them, you are then ready to go on with the rest of your story. Rewrite each paragraph several times until you get it right. End your story with a paragraph that summarizes what your subject is all about. A good example that shows how the end should relate to the beginning is in the Crow's Mill story included at the end of this chapter.

Footnotes

Every direct quote, every fact taken from a source, every opinion that is not yours should be credited to the source from which it came. The method used for such credit is the footnote.

Your English grammar book will give you detailed instructions on what a footnote contains and the form of footnotes.

Bibliography

The bibliography should appear at the end of your story. It should contain only the materials that have been used for reference in your writing. The bibliography should be arranged in alphabetical order, by authors, with last names first. (See Chapter 3 for sample formats.)

Your Final Story

After you have finished writing your story, you can share it with other people. Many stories written by young people have been published in state historical magazines and are now secondary sources of local history. You may want to put your story into a notebook and illustrate it with photographs, excerpts from old letters and journals or copies of old newspaper headlines. Your notebook might be added to your city or town library's local history collection, or to your school library's collection. But no matter where it ends up, you can be proud of the fact that you have helped to record and preserve part of American history.

Student Local History Projects

Crow's Mill School

by Jenny Murray
Glenwood Junior High School, Chatham, Illinois
(Excerpted from *Illinois History*, Oct. 1981)

Reading and 'riting and 'rithmetic
Taught to the tune of a hickory stick . . .

This tune sometimes goes through my mind when I ride my bicycle past the Crow's Mill School, A Unique Tavern, and think of how it must have been years ago when it was a rural schoolhouse.

Now, in 1981, the sounds of jazz, rock, blues and country music can be heard from the open windows and doors as many college students and other people in the community enjoy the food and entertainment of today's Crow's Mill School.

The Crow's Mill School is in my neighborhood. The building is located at the corner of Toronto Road and Crow's Mill Lane just south of Springfield and north of Lake Springfield. I have often passed by this building on my way to school. My school bus driver, Mrs. Phyllis White, said she had attended Crow's Mill School years ago, but it had not been in that location. I became interested in its past, so I went to Lincoln Library in Springfield. There I found information and pictures in the Sangamon Valley Collection, a section on the third floor of the library which has information about the history of Sangamon County. Through old newspaper articles and an old map of area schools, I found out that Mrs. White was right about Crow's Mill School being in a different location. It had been built approximately three-fourths of a mile south of its present site.

The original Crow's Mill School was built nearly one hundred years ago on land which is now part of Lake Springfield. The school derived its name from a nearby flour mill, Crow's Mill, which was named after Robert Crow who built the mill in 1825–1826.

In 1933, when Lake Springfield was built, the old school was moved to its present site on Toronto Road, and a brick veneer was added. Another school, named South Crow's Mill, was built about four miles south of the first Crow's Mill School, and accommodated pupils south of the lake. Several generations of area families have attended classes in the old North Crow's Mill and South Crow's Mill schools. In 1957, North Crow's Mill School had fifty-one pupils in six grades. Teachers were Miss Susan Flagg of Sherman, who taught at the school for twenty-two years, and Mrs. Alta Claypool of Williamsville, who had been there for six years.

In March, 1957, the time of one- and two-room country schoolhouses in Sangamon County came to an end when the doors of four little schools in Community Unit District 5 closed. At that time pupils attending North Crow's Mill, South Crow's Mill, New City and Glenarm schools were transferred to the old Ball Township High School, located in the eastern half of Ball-Chatham School District. High school students had moved into a new structure, Glenwood High School, on Chatham Road earlier in March, 1957.

After the North Crow's Mill School closed its doors as a school, it became the Navy Club, a local tavern. A boat and anchor could be seen on the lawn during those years.

In about 1977, the Navy Club was purchased by a group of people interested in restoring the building to look like the original school. It is now called Crow's Mill School, a Unique Tavern. The boat and anchor are gone and a new sign with a big black crow is on the building. Inside are the same hardwood floors that young pupils walked on years ago. Pictures on the walls show groups of students who attended the school. The three Rs of "reading, 'riting, and 'rithmetic" are no longer taught in this building, but instead it is now a place of recreation and relaxation for people in the area.

Jenny Murray's sources:

Illinois State Journal (Springfield), April 22, 1974, p. 13; State Register (Springfield), March 21, 1957, p. 31; County Superintendent of Schools, Sangamon County, Illinois, Map of School Districts; interviews with Mrs. Phyllis White, Glenarm; Jack Day, Chatham; and Baze Reinders, Springfield.

From Past to Present

by Laurie Pearsall, Wendy Barry and Laura Murphy
Mount Olive High School, Flanders, New Jersey
(Excerpts from a notebook prepared by the authors.)

On December 17, 1760, Jabez Heaton bought a tract of 562 acres of land from William Allen of Philadelphia. William Allen had bought an 1100-acre tract in North Jersey from William Penn.

After moving to Mendham in 1756, John Ayers bought 19 acres from Jabez Heaton. On these 19 acres the village of Old Flanders still stands. Among the earliest of the settlers in Flanders was Jonathan Nicholas. His son, Rhece Nicholas, married the daughter of John Ayers, Elizabeth. The Nicholas family and the Ed McLaughlins were the primary educators of the earliest settlers in Flanders.

With about 50 houses in a one-mile radius, Flanders was at one time the largest settlement in the township. As the population grew, farming increased; surrounding hills were full of iron-ore mines. This industry helped the thriving community. During outbreaks of the War for Independence, the iron-ore was used to manufacture shells for rifles. There was a shell factory in the area which is now referred to as "East Tin Cup" on North Road.

The years from 1827 to 1859 were known as the "boom" period for this area. Farming and mining provided many prosperous jobs for the people in this settlement.

At one time, Flanders had freight trains, blacksmiths, two creameries, three grist mills, two post offices, three general stores, two sand pits, two butchers, and a fish peddler, along with about 100 farms. The churches, stores, post offices, and railroad stations were the usual gathering places.

The two most important roads in Flanders during the 1800s were the Boston Post Road and the old road from Succasunna to Long Valley.

This old town was once called the "Ice Box of New Jersey." The nickname originated because as many as six freight trains a day passed through Flanders, bringing ice to New York for refrigeration.

Because new laws have been created to prevent the modernization of this town, many of the original buildings are still standing. Residents of this community recognize the historical value of Flanders and have agreed that this environment should be preserved.

The Flanders Post Office:

In 1822, the Flanders Post Office was organized. Mr. Rhece Nicholas was elected as a postmaster in 1925. He was elected simply because he was the only resident who could read and write. The letters cost 10 cents apiece and no stamps were used. The post office was stationed in . . . buildings . . . directly across from one another on Main Street.

The Story of the Old Rock Church*

by Deborah L. Klingmann
Dobie Junior High School, Austin, Texas
(Excerpted from *Texas Historian*, Vol. XLIII, May 1983.
Courtesy of the Texas State Historical Association.)

The Civil War had begun, and the winter had been severe, but the men of the church, along with their slaves, went to Bastrop to get timber and other supplies needed for the building. Dodging Indians and crossing streams were the most difficult aspects of the journey. Many ruts had to be filled and many trees cut down for the wagons to travel these trails safely. The wagons were drawn by oxen, and some of the men followed on foot. The congregation brought the rock for the building. The walls were made eighteen inches thick. With much work and effort, the building was finally completed at a cost of $700.00. These walls remain as part of the present facilities of the church.

Indians remained a threat for some years, so it was necessary for the men to carry their rifles to church for protection. One man would stand outside the door to warn of a possible Indian attack, although there is no record that such an attack ever took place.

After the Civil War a series of depressions occurred, which left nearly everyone poorer. In 1882, a storm blew the roof off the Old Rock Church. Church members were unable to replace it, probably due to lack of funds. For the next two and a half years services were held in the old Summit School, but finally the roof was repaired for $133.10.

There is a story that around the turn of the century, three bandits robbed the M-K-T train near McNeil. The robbers came upon the Old Rock Church and spent the night there. The next morning the sheriff picked up their trail and chased them as far as Liberty Hill, shooting two of the men. One was killed and the other was injured. The two surviving bandits went to prison for thirty years. The injured man died while in prison. When the last of the three was set free, he returned to the community to dig up the buried loot. He stopped at the Fiskville store, told the owner about the robbery, and inquired about a rock schoolhouse near a creek where they buried the money. The storekeeper mentioned the Fiskville School, but that was not the place. He then mentioned a rock church just up the road. The bandit said he would split the money with the church if they would help him find it. (In those days, when a robber hid his loot and served his time in prison, it was legally his after he was freed, provided it had not already been found. Supposedly, he had paid for it by having served his time.) The store owner referred him to Mr. Neans. Several days later the store owner saw Neans and asked him whether the man had contacted him yet. When Neans replied that he had not, the two went to investigate and found the hole and the iron skillet in which the money had been buried. The bottom of the skillet had round, corroded marks the size of silver coins. This story has become something of a legend, but Neans was an eyewitness.

When the church was first built, candles were used for lighting. Some of these candles hung on the walls, with reflectors behind them. A chandelier held twenty or thirty more candles, which hung from the ceiling. The last man to leave the building would fan the candles with his hat to put them out.

One of the oldest private cemeteries in Travis County is found on the grounds of the Walnut Creek Church. The graves near the back of the cemetery, with unmarked rocks as headstones, probably belong to slaves. At the foot of Henry Neans's grave is the headstone of his faithful dog, Watch, who was buried near him at Neans's request. The grave of George V. Barnes, son of Charles and Elizabeth Barnes, may be the oldest grave. He died in 1861 at the age of twenty-two, possibly a Civil War victim. Charles and Elizabeth, two of the charter members of the church, are buried in the same plot. There are many infant graves and stones bearing the names of many families well known to the community.

Deborah Klingmann's sources:

Adrian W. Coleman, *Upon This Rock*, 1952; Kenneth Thompson, *The History of the Old Rock Church*, 1981; Joe West, *A Century of Christianity in a Christ-Centered Church*, 1957; Jack E. Beck, "Walnut Creek Baptist Church Celebrates 110th Anniversary," 1966; Dora Dieterich Bonham, "Walnut Creek Baptist Church," Travis County, Texas," 1965; The Austin Baptist Association Annual Minutes, 1982; and Interview with Ruth Cearley, 1981.

*The church once known as the "Old Rock Church" is the Walnut Creek Baptist Church in Austin, Texas.

Directory

This directory gives you more places to look for information as well as people to contact. The information can lead you to many different sources to help you complete your story.

If You Need:

An address or a telephone number of a historical society

Here's What You Do:

Look in the library for a directory titled *Directory of Historical Societies and Agencies*, Donna McDonald, editor and compiler. It is published by the American Association for State and Local History; 1400 8th Avenue, South; Nashville, Tennessee 37203. See also *The Writer's Resource Guide* as follows.

An address or a telephone number of a library, museum or historical society	Look in the library for a book titled *The Writer's Resource Guide,* by William Brohaugh. Published by Writer's Digest Books. Not all the available resources are listed, however.
An address or a telephone number of an organization, as well as the history of the organization	Find a book titled *Encyclopedia of Associations,* Denis S. Akey, editor. Issued yearly, the book is published by Gale Research Co., Detroit, Michigan. Available at most public libraries in the research section.
Information about the National Park Service and its local history programs	Write to the Superintendent of Documents, U.S. Government Printing Office, Washington, D.C. 20402. Ask for a booklet titled *Living History in the National Park System* and for booklets that cover historic sites in your state.
Information from the National Archives	Write to the National Archives, Central Reference Division, General Services Administration, Washington, D.C. 20408. Your letter will be routed to the correct office.

Oral history tapes

Look in your public library's reference section for a book titled *Oral History in the United States, A Directory,* compiled by Gary L. Schumway. Published by The Oral History Association, New York. Look in libraries for oral history directories. Descriptions of tapes are arranged alphabetically by the name of the city, then by the name of the project. County and subject indexes are included. At the end of each listing is a contact name of the person or institution from whom you can borrow the tape. A postage fee is charged. Ask for the librarian's help if you can't find these directories or if you don't understand the information in them.

Index